RICK

LOKI

BARKIE

WOLF

AURORA

FOX

JACK

STEVE

FRANCIS

CURLY

PHILIP

HAMLET

HOTDOG

AKIRA

ELFIE

SONYA

MASHA

WOOSTER

FOR ALYOSHA
and everyone else

A huge thank you to my wonderful
dog models: Pina, Bruce, Reyna, Ashi,
Jim, Baikal, Alma, Jake, Vetrusha,
Shu, Hanna, Jenny, Batman, Dana,
Atlanta, Yusta, Zeev, Shastik, Zoyka,
Marty, Livey, Loki, Ding Dong, Nayda,
Pepper, Miroslava, Milka, Iris, Lyalya,
Shani, Dominique, Teddy, Pixel, Nila,
Heathcliff, Tosha, Patrick, Bumblebee,
Sava, Kasya, Masha, Thunder, Bonya,
Terry, Zunita, Mercy, Archer, Florida,
Lusha, Yuki, Akela, Jasper, Elf, Hamlet,
Akira, Wooster, Philip, Francis, Aurora,
Fly, and to their owners, who sent me
their photos.

I also want to thank Alexander K.,
who helped me to sort (well, he just
did it for me) through hundreds of
emails and thousands of dog photos.
I couldn't have done it without him!

HOW TO BE YOUR DOG'S BEST FRIEND

WRITTEN AND ILLUSTRATED BY ELENA BULAY

TRANSLATED FROM THE RUSSIAN BY LENA TRAER

HELLO!
MY NAME IS LENA

I'm not a dog trainer, I'm an illustrator.
I have a dog named Jo and we live
in Moscow. When I got her, I hardly
knew anything about dogs, so I made
a lot of mistakes. I hope this book will
help you to understand what dogs are
like, how to communicate with them,
and how to take care of them.

AND THIS IS JO
My favorite dog
and best friend

CONTENTS

THERE ARE SO MANY DIFFERENT DOGS!

There are so many different kinds of dogs in the world! Dogs with long legs and short legs. Long droopy ears and pointy ears, big floppy ears and button ears. They can be extremely fluffy or even bald! White, black, brown, foxy red, golden, speckled, spotted, you name it.

MOP-LIKE

GROOMED

CURLY-HAIRED

SHORT-LEGGED

TEENY TINY

SCRUFFY

ROUND

SKINNY

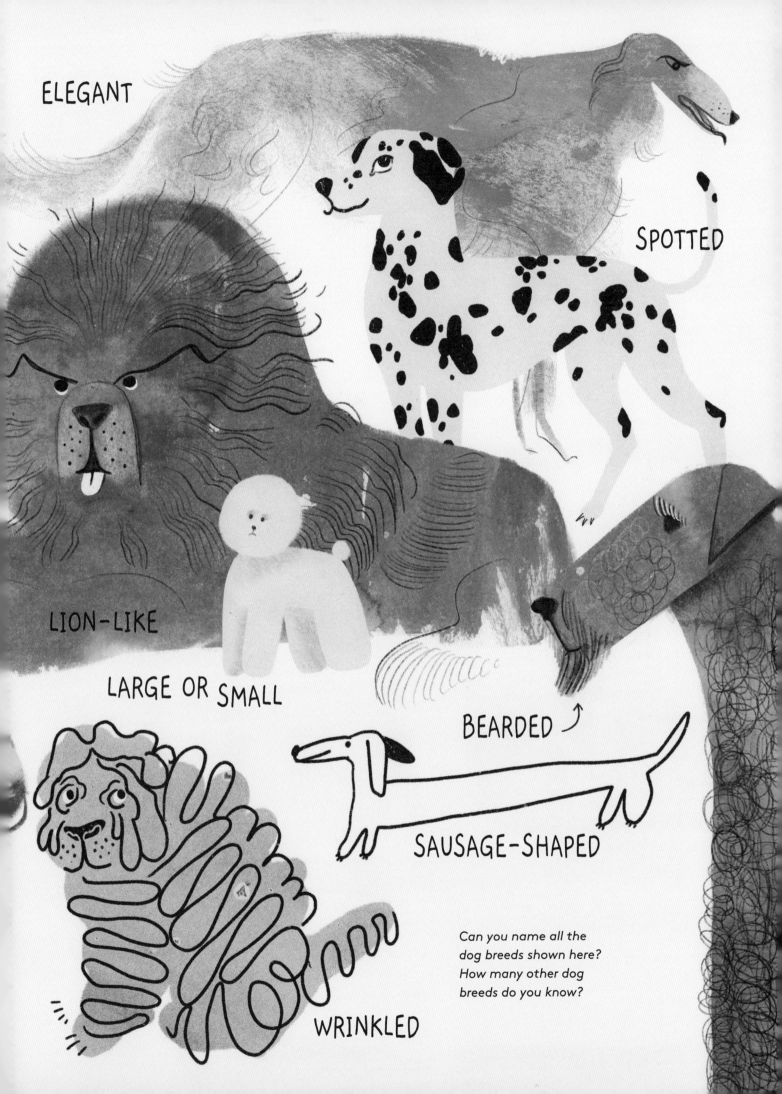

ELEGANT

SPOTTED

LION-LIKE

LARGE OR SMALL

BEARDED ↱

SAUSAGE-SHAPED

Can you name all the
dog breeds shown here?
How many other dog
breeds do you know?

WRINKLED

Short brown eyelashes

Soft velvety ears, the tips are almost always floppy

Intelligent brown eyes, it looks like she's wearing eyeliner

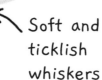
Soft and ticklish whiskers

Wet black nose (sometimes dry)

6 years old

Pink heart-shaped spots on her nose ♥

There are stiff whiskers on her chin too

Big white teeth (you can't see them now)

Jo

Long claws because Jo doesn't like having them trimmed

Cute little heels

21 inches tall (to shoulder)

44 inches from the tip of her nose to the tip of her tail

231 black spots

Fluffy tail

Pink tummy with black spots. Jo likes it when I rub it.

43 brown spots

Weighs **49** lbs

MY DOG IS THE BEST!

Jo is six years old. I don't know who her mother or father were, but she turned out to be smart and beautiful. She is a pretty large dog. She is taller than my knee and weighs just over forty-nine pounds.

When I got Jo, she was white with brown-black ears. But later, it was as if tiny black and brown spots began to jump from her ears across to her back and paws. More and more spots keep appearing. One day, this white dog might turn completely black—wouldn't that be something?

WHERE TO GET A DOG

The basenji is one of the oldest dog breeds in the world. It first appeared thousands of years ago in Central Africa. In ancient Egypt, dogs that look like basenjis appeared in wall paintings and other art. Unusually, basenjis don't bark: instead they growl or make a yodeling sound.

Dogs have lived with humans for thousands of years. As a species, they originated from wolves. Even though all dogs have a common ancestor, they vary greatly in size and shape—worldwide, there are around 370 officially recognized dog breeds. Some of them are ancient; others have only recently been added to the list. There are hunting dogs, gun dogs, sled dogs, herding dogs, fighting dogs, toy dogs, and companion dogs. Each breed has its own distinctive features. Some have webbed feet for swimming, some are super-fast runners, others are sweet-natured and gentle.

If your family wants a purebred (or pedigree) dog, you will need to find a breeder. How do you know you've found a good one? A good breeder will have a long track record of breeding dogs of one or just a few breeds, and will have taken part in shows or competitions. A good breeder will ask you and your family plenty of questions to make sure their puppy is going to a good home. When you come to see the puppy, the breeder will show you where their dogs live. You'll be able to check how comfortable they are and whether they feel safe there. A good breeder also knows the personalities of their puppies, and will provide you with all the necessary documents. They should be able to offer advice about care and training, and will usually be willing to take the puppy back if you are unable to care for them.

A great alternative is to adopt a rescue dog. Some of these dogs were born as strays and taken in, some were lost or abandoned, and others were given up because their owner died or wasn't able to look after them any more. At dog shelters and rescue centers, you can find both puppies and adult dogs. Sometimes you can find purebred dogs there, but many rescue dogs are mixed breeds. They are all different, with their own, often sad, stories, but all of these dogs need new friends and a new home.

The very first dog shelter was opened in Japan in 1695. The dogs were kept at the government's expense and fed a choice diet of rice and dried fish.

Dog shelters can house anything from a dozen to hundreds of animals, but they should all be kept in good conditions.

Spending time with rescue dogs, training and socializing them, keeps them happy and gives them a better chance of finding a new permanent home.

A dog's life in a shelter is not ideal. It's common for several dogs to share one kennel. The shelter staff takes good care of the dogs: they feed them, give them any medical treatments they need, and spend as much time with them as they can. But there are sometimes lots of dogs and not enough staff. For this reason, volunteers often help out at shelters, and give the dogs the walks and human company they need. If your family is not sure about getting a pet, you could try volunteering at a rescue center near where you live—you can visit the dogs there, give them attention, and take them out for exercise.

Some people also try to help animals on their own. They pick up dogs and cats on the streets, take them in, make sure they get necessary medical treatment, and then try to find them a new home.

I've wanted a dog ever since I was a child, but for a long time I couldn't bring myself to get one because a dog is a living thing. You need to take them out for walks, feed them, and take care of them. I worried that I wouldn't be able to handle it. But one day I decided—it's now or never!

I decided that I wanted to adopt a rescue dog—there are too many homeless dogs who need someone to care for them. I started to read website posts and message boards every day, looking for MY dog.

HOW TO CHOOSE A DOG

The saddest thing that can happen is when a dog is not a good fit for their new family. Too often, when people choose a dog, they only think about how the dog looks. That's not enough. Dogs not only come in different shapes and sizes, but their personalities, energy levels, and needs are different too. First, you need to think about the kind of dog that will be a good match for you and your family. Ask yourself these questions:

How much time can you spend walking your dog on weekdays and weekends?

Is anyone in your family allergic to dogs?

Do you and your family lead active lives? Do you like walking? Do you cycle a lot or go hiking? Do you want a dog with lots of energy? Or would you prefer a calm companion who likes to stay at home?

Where do you live? In an apartment or in a house with a garden or yard? Is there a park, a forest, or a dog play area nearby?

Some dogs are more high-maintenance than others. They need a lot of grooming to keep their coat in good condition. Does your family have enough time to spend on walking, grooming, and playing with a dog?

Who will take your dog for walks? Large dogs need to be walked by an adult.

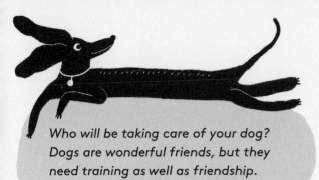

Who will be taking care of your dog? Dogs are wonderful friends, but they need training as well as friendship.

Can your family afford a dog? Bigger dogs need more food. You'll also need to buy equipment and toys, and pay for vaccinations and medical treatment if the dog gets sick.

How often do you go on vacation? Will you be able to take the dog with you, or will you leave them with friends or relatives or at a boarding kennel while you're away?

Why do you want a dog? How will they fit into your family's life? What dog personality is right for you? Every breed and every individual dog has their own characteristics and needs. Will you be able to meet those needs, and will they match yours? And the most important question of all—will you be happy with each other?

THINGS TO THINK ABOUT

Whether you decide to get a purebred puppy or a rescue dog, talk with the breeder or shelter staff to learn as much about the dog as possible.

- What kind of personality does the dog have? Does this breed have any special traits? Is there anything you need to watch out for in the future? If you are getting a dog from a shelter, try to find out about their past if possible. Do they have behavior issues? What should you be prepared for?

- Is the dog healthy? If the dog is purebred, find out everything you can about the health of the puppy and their parents.

- Has the dog been treated for fleas, ticks, and worms? Are their vaccinations up to date? When you adopt a dog from a shelter, you'll need to take them to the vet for a health check.

- What does the puppy eat? Do the breeders or shelter staff have a diet sheet to take home with you, telling you what to feed the dog and how much? Talk to a vet about recommended foods.

- Does the dog seem scared or aggressive? If so, when does this happen? Does the dog get along with other dogs? What about other animals?

- Are they male or female? Different genders of dog may behave differently. If they are a purebred dog, do you want to breed puppies? If they are a rescue dog, have they been neutered?

One day, I was randomly browsing a website where they sell or give away things for free, and I came across an ad for Jo! Although she wasn't called Jo yet—she was just a white puppy with no name.

Puppy seeking a new family!

Free to a good home. Please call

This is Julia. She found Jo on the street, arranged a foster home for her, and started looking for a new family to adopt her.

Julia often looks after dogs and cats and finds new homes for them

This is me, wearing a raincoat because it's cold and drizzling in late September. A few months later, Jo chewed through my coat pockets.

First to the metro...

I called the number in the ad. The person who answered turned out to run a dog shelter. She asked me a lot of questions about why I wanted a dog and whether I'd be able to take care of her. It felt like a real exam! The next day, I went over for a meet-and-greet. Jo was staying in a foster home* at a vet's house in the countryside.

I took the train for an hour or longer,
I don't quite remember...

It felt like a long time...

Then I got off at a station...

Then to the train station...

...and I took the bus for another forty minutes or so. I was afraid I might miss the village I needed.

This is where Jo lived, with several other dogs.

* A foster home is a place where rescue dogs can live until they are adopted by a new family.

There were other dogs at the vet's house as well as Jo: five young, playful black mixed-breed dogs, two sad-looking adult dogs that were also waiting for new families, and a huge older dog that belonged to the vet. The vet introduced me to everyone and asked if I'd take one of the black puppies. No one ever picks them—perhaps people don't think they're cute. But I had come for Jo and I wanted to see her!

Finally she came out—a skinny little dog, long and white, with knobbly knees. Quiet and cautious. I didn't know what to do. We stood facing each other. It was drizzling. I stretched out my hand, and she sniffed it.

PREPARING YOUR HOME

WALKING HARNESS

Dogs can hurt their necks from pulling or tugging on the leash. Make sure that the harness fits properly and doesn't rub your dog's skin. Choose a harness designed to suit your dog's body.

P. 48

COLLAR

Your dog should always wear a collar, even at home. The ID tag is attached to the collar.

LEASH

Fifteen-foot leash for long walks
Six-foot leash for shorter walks

DOG BED

Find a quiet, calm place to put the bed—somewhere your dog can sleep, chew on toys, and feel safe. You can use a special dog bed with a removable cover, or just a pile of warm blankets, as long as the bedding can be easily washed.

BOWLS

Use stainless steel or ceramic bowls. You should wash your pet's bowls after every meal.

ID TAG

This is very important! If a dog gets lost, an ID tag means that they can be returned home. Your dog's name is engraved on one side, and your phone number on the other.

DOG POOP BAGS

Always clean up after your dog. You can buy special pet waste bags in pet stores and supermarkets.

SHAMPOO

Human shampoo is not good for dogs! You will need a special one.

NAIL CLIPPERS

For trimming your dog's claws

BRUSH

You should brush your dog, otherwise when they are shedding, their hair will be all over your floor and furniture.

FIRST AID KIT

If your dog gets sick or injured, some basic first aid supplies are essential.

COTTON

ORHEXIDINE

Hydrogen
Peroxide

MUZZLE

Even if you have a very gentle dog, you might sometimes need a muzzle for rides on public transit or visits to the vet.

TOYS

Dogs love to play. It's a good way to learn new things. There are even special enrichment toys with treats hidden inside. Toys can also be made from things you may already have around the house.

Dogs love to chew. That's why they need bones too.

p. 53

PADS

If your puppy or adult dog is not yet house trained, you'll need to teach them to go on a puppy pad first.

p. 42

I bought a leash and some bowls, and made a dog bed out of an old bathrobe. Then I waited. They brought Jo over in a car and gave her to me outside, in the courtyard. She sat down and wouldn't budge. I had to pick her up to carry her indoors. And she wasn't a small puppy by then—she weighed twenty-six pounds!

YOUR DOG'S NEW HOME

Once your dog comes home for the first time, you'll want to cuddle and play with them right away. It's best not to do that, however. Let your dog adjust first. Whether they're a puppy or an adult dog, everything will seem new, strange, and scary—new people, new spaces, new things, smells, and sounds.

Every dog is different, so their reactions might be different too. One dog might eagerly start exploring, sniffing every corner, and meeting everyone. Another might freeze at first, then take a while to investigate and get used to their new home.

Prepare your home in advance. Look around and try to work out what a puppy can reach. Put away anything valuable and hide your shoes, power cords, and toys. Move plants to where the puppy can't get to them. Chewing is very normal for dogs, so it's likely that a few things will get destroyed. Get some dog toys for your puppy to chew on.

p. 55

Show your dog their water bowl and bed—then leave them alone for a few hours. Go about your day as usual. Let the dog get used to you and their new home slowly. When the dog starts showing an interest in you, hold out your hand, let them sniff it, and start talking to them. After a few hours, you can take them out for a walk, if it's safe to do so.

If you have something from the dog's previous home, place it on their bed. A toy, or perhaps a blanket with a familiar smell. This will make it easier for the dog to get settled in.

p. 33

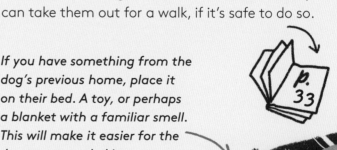

26

HOW DO DOGS COMMUNICATE?

Do they bark or growl? Do they sometimes howl or whimper? Yes, they do communicate that way, but they mainly use body language. If you know your dog well, you will immediately understand when they're having fun and when they're sad, afraid of something, or stressed. With only their eyes and facial expression they can say, "Give me that piece of cheese! I want it so much!"

Dogs can bark and growl in different ways. It can be a warning growl—"don't come near me!", or a happy growl—"come on, let's play, why are you so slow!" It all depends on how the dog behaves at that moment, and what their body language tells us.

To be your dog's best friend, you will need to learn the language they use to communicate—body language! Watch their tail and ears, their facial expressions, and their body postures.

See the next page for the most common body positions and what they mean.

Wrong

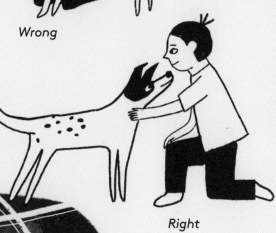

Right

Everyone loves to hug dogs. But in general, dogs don't like to be hugged. If someone is towering over them and hugging them, not letting them go, they often perceive it as a threat. And sometimes dogs bite! However, they almost never bite without a reason or a warning. It's just that we don't understand their language that well. Before biting, a dog may ask us to stop bothering them: turn their head away, lick their lips slowly or very fast, flatten their ears, try to get away, or warn us with a low growl. They usually bite only if we ignore all of those signals.

A dog is not a toy. They are a member of your family just like everyone else. Sometimes your dog can be in a bad mood, can suffer from pain, or may just want to lay quietly and be left alone.

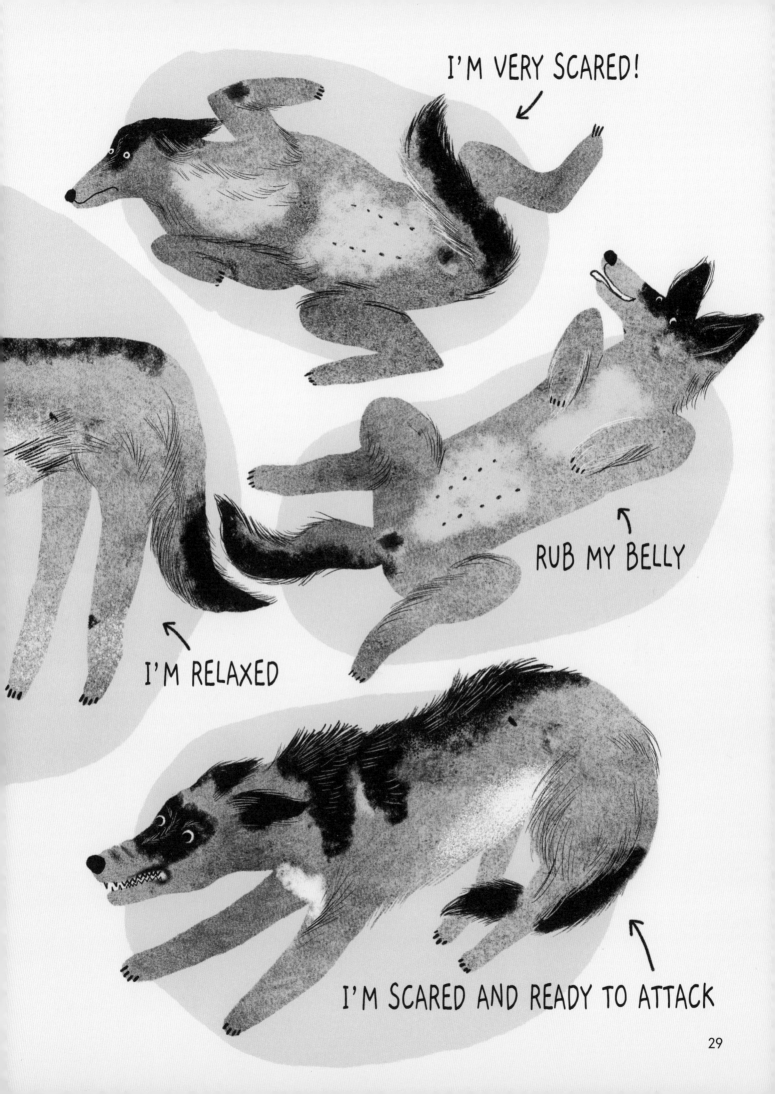

Some people make new friends easily, but others need more time. The same is true for dogs. Jo and I are both aloof, so it took us a while to become friends. When I brought Jo home, she was afraid to go into rooms, so she spent the night in the hallway. I moved her dog bed close to the door. I couldn't fall asleep for a long time. I kept listening for her breathing. The next few days, Jo cautiously explored the apartment. I talked to her, played with her, and gave her treats—that's how we got to know each other.

For the first six months, Jo did not make a sound. She was the quietest dog in the world! To be honest, I thought she couldn't bark. Imagine my surprise, when one day I was working in my studio and suddenly heard a deep loud woof! That's how long it took her to get comfortable with me. Now Jo is a very talkative dog.

IMPORTANT ITEMS

OWNER
FIRST AND LAST NAME

ADDRESS

DESCRIPTION OF ANIMAL

NAME

DATE OF BIRTH   SEX

COLOR

BREED

COAT
NOTABLE OR DISCERNIBLE FEATURES OR CHARACTERISTICS

BREEDER

Some pet passports include a full-body photo, but others have only a head portrait.

Depending on where you live, dog passports may look different and will have different covers, but their contents are usually pretty similar.

PASSPORT OR MEDICAL CERTIFICATE

If you want to take your dog abroad, you will need a pet passport or medical certificate. It shows that your dog is healthy, is fit to take part in shows and competitions, and can travel. It also contains a description of your dog, a record of their vaccinations, and details about their microchip (see the opposite page).

The specific documents that you will need vary according to the country you live in and the country you are traveling to, so be sure to check the rules carefully before you go. To enter the U.S., for instance, your dog will need a rabies vaccination certificate if the country you are traveling from has a high risk of rabies.

VACCINATIONS

When puppies are born, they feed on their mother's milk. The milk contains antibodies that protect them and help to keep them healthy. When puppies start eating other foods, these antibodies gradually disappear. This is why your dog needs to be vaccinated. Usually a series of shots is given by a vet before a puppy turns one. The first vaccines are given when the puppy is eight to nine weeks old.

Before the first vaccination and for several weeks afterward, while immunity develops, you should keep your dog at home: they should not take walks outside or meet other dogs, because they are still at risk of catching a disease. If the vaccinations are delayed for some reason, you might need to talk to a dog behaviorist: spending too long in quarantine can be bad for your dog.

Follow-up vaccines are given within a certain time period, usually once a year, but sometimes less frequently. Always consult a vet about the details.

Talk to your vet about a schedule for vaccinations. Make sure to deworm your dog seven to ten days before a shot. A healthy dog will be less likely to suffer side effects from the vaccine.

The chip is injected under the skin over the shoulder blades

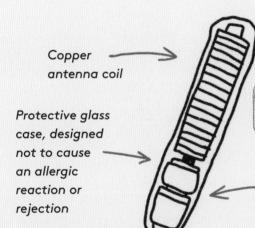

Copper antenna coil

Actual size of microchip

Protective glass case, designed not to cause an allergic reaction or rejection

Tuning capacitor and microchip

MICROCHIP

A microchip is a little computer chip inside a tiny glass case, roughly the size of a grain of rice. It's inserted under your dog's skin with a special needle. It is basically an electronic passport: when the chip is scanned, it shows a unique identification number. This information is recorded on a database run by the chip manufacturer, along with the dog owner's contact details. If a dog gets lost, a microchip means they have a much better chance of being reunited with their owners. In the U.S., the microchipping of dogs is only required by law in the state of Hawaii, but vets strongly recommend it.

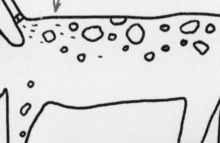

The first animal microchip implants were introduced in the Netherlands in 1989.

The chip number has fifteen digits:

643 0981 00000003

country code or manufacturer code

manufacturer code

individual code

After a life of danger on the street, Jo made it into a foster home and then to me. I got her vaccinated and kept her indoors for a while—Jo hadn't been outside for over a month. Our first walk was terrible. Jo was scared to leave the apartment, then to leave the lobby, and once she was out in the street, she shrank with fear and refused to move. She was afraid of everything!

At first, I would take her out for a walk around the courtyard, then slowly expanded our route. Little by little, I trained Jo to get used to new things: to walk into a store, to pass close to a car, to wait at a traffic light, to cross the street.

It took several months. But Jo learned to cope! She is still a scaredy-cat, but she is now brave enough to enjoy her walks and meet other dogs and people.

FEEDING YOUR DOG

Dogs are predators. And what do predators eat? You've got it, raw meat! That's why a dog's diet mainly consists of meat. But a complete and balanced diet should also include other foods, containing proteins, fats, carbohydrates, vitamins, and minerals. There are two main types of dog food: commercial dog food and homemade food.

The dry pet food industry started in 1860. After traveling to London to sell lightning rods, an American electrician named James Spratt noticed street dogs eating moldy biscuits thrown away by sailors. He formulated the first dog biscuit: a mix of blended wheat, vegetables, beetroot, and beef blood. The biscuits were expensive, and, at first, were mainly bought by wealthy gentlemen to feed their hunting dogs.

Grate vegetables or cut them into bite-sized pieces.

COMMERCIAL DOG FOOD

Commercial dog food is specially made to contain everything that dogs need. It comes in dry (kibble) or wet (canned) forms.

• You should always choose a dog food that's designed to provide the best nutrition. Cheaper dog foods contain mostly grains and not much meat, which is not a healthy option for your dog.

• When choosing dog food, read the label first. The ingredients are listed by weight, starting with the heaviest. Good-quality dog foods will have different types of meat or meat products at the top, followed by vegetables, fruits, oils, various supplements, and vitamins. Grains should be listed toward the end and should not exceed 10 percent of the contents.

• Puppies, senior dogs, and sick dogs need specially designed dog foods because their needs are different.

Once a week, you can try giving your dog a boiled egg.

HOMEMADE DOG FOOD

Homemade food does not mean feeding your dog table scraps and kitchen leftovers—things like spaghetti and meatballs or chicken soup. It means preparing special meals for your dog, which should always include protein. The hardest part is coming up with a meal plan that provides enough nutrition. A balanced diet includes:

- Meat (beef, pork), poultry (turkey, chicken), fish (hake, cod, halibut, pollock)—roughly half of the food should be from this category.
- Low-fat cultured dairy products.
- Vegetables (zucchini, pumpkin, cucumber, pepper, celery, cauliflower, broccoli, carrot, green beans), fruits (apple, banana, pear, melon), berries, leafy greens.
- Cereals in small amounts (buckwheat, rice, rolled oats, bran).

Talk to a vet about whether you should give your dog vitamins.

Dogs have been fed some strange things over the years! In the nineteenth century, Dowager Empress Cixi of China fed her Pekingese dogs on quail breasts and shark fins, with antelope milk to drink.

Add a little olive or sunflower oil—just a few drops or a spoonful, depending on the size of the dog.

When you feed your dog fish or chicken, make sure to remove all bones.

When choosing dog food or creating a home-cooked meal plan, talk to a vet or a dog nutritionist.

Feed a puppy four to five times a day at first. Then gradually cut down the number of meals to two to three times a day by the time they're one year old.

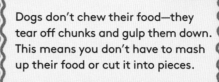

Dogs don't chew their food—they tear off chunks and gulp them down. This means you don't have to mash up their food or cut it into pieces.

HOW OFTEN SHOULD DOGS EAT AND HOW MUCH?

When buying dog food in a store, look at the instructions on the label. Portion size varies based on your dog's breed, weight, and age.

With homemade meals, approximate daily food intake should be 3.5 percent of their body weight, or 7 percent of body weight for puppies under six months old. But it depends on the specific needs of the dog, their age, energy levels, and general health.

Your dog should never get more than 10 percent of their daily food from treats. These contain lots of calories and overfeeding your dog isn't a good idea. Treats can be rewards during training sessions or just for fun. You can buy them at a pet store or make them at home.

An adult dog should eat twice a day, in the morning and in the evening, always at the same time after a walk.

HOW MUCH WATER DOES A DOG NEED?

On average, dogs need one ounce of water per pound of body weight each day. They may drink more or less than that, depending on the food they eat. Make sure your dog always has plenty of clean water. Change the water at least once a day.

Take raw beef liver, wash it under running cold water, and cut it into small cubes (around half an inch). Space out the liver cubes on a baking tray, lined with parchment paper. Bake at a very low heat (under 200°F) for several hours, until they turn dry and crispy.

FORBIDDEN FOODS FOR DOGS

CHOCOLATE

Chocolate contains a chemical called theobromine, which is toxic to dogs. Even a small piece of chocolate can cause vomiting, diarrhea, and a racing heart. Large amounts may cause heart failure and death.

GRAPES AND RAISINS

Grapes and raisins (dried grapes) are very toxic to dogs. Even a small amount can cause kidney failure.

AVOCADO

Avocados contain a toxin called persin. This can cause vomiting and diarrhea in dogs.

ONIONS AND GARLIC

Onions and garlic contain chemical compounds that can destroy red blood cells and lead to anemia.

IS IT SAFE TO GIVE TABLE SCRAPS TO YOUR DOG?

A dog's digestive system is different from a human's. Most human food is too rich and fatty for a dog to digest. It contains more carbohydrates, less protein, and large amounts of salt, sugar, and spices. This rich diet can lead to serious health problems in your dog, so it's a bad idea to feed your dog table scraps. But the occasional treat is still okay: your pet will love small pieces of fresh vegetables, fruits, berries, salad greens, lean meat, nuts, and a tiny bit of cheese. Many dogs love cheese, but since it is high in fat, you should avoid giving them too much of it.

When I got Jo, she was skinny as a beanpole. It seemed like I could count her ribs. Concerned passers-by would stop me in the street and tell me to feed my dog more.

At the same time, Jo would always wolf down her meals in seconds. She practically inhaled them! But she kept growing. She shot up right before my eyes, yet still somehow stayed very thin.

What's more, Jo was a sneaky little thief!

One day, I cooked a whole pot of chicken curry. I took off the cover to let the curry cool down a bit and left the kitchen for five minutes or so. When I came back, I couldn't believe my eyes: the pot on the stove was clean as a whistle. There was no curry left in it! Not a drop!

Next to the stove sat Jo—all sleepy, lazily smacking her lips. She looked at me in a dazed way. "That was a heavenly curry!" she seemed to say.

ALL DOGS DO IT

Dogs pee and poop just like humans. But while we can use a toilet, dogs need to go outside. Dogs are neat animals. They naturally get used to relieving themselves outside, but this habit forms at different ages. Some puppies can hold it between toilet breaks at four to five months old, others start doing this at the age of ten to twelves months.

Sometimes an adult dog has an "accident" indoors. There can be many different reasons for this—perhaps not enough walks, or the walks are not long enough. The dog might also be stressed or sick. If your dog suddenly starts peeing inside, see a vet. If they are healthy, think about what might be causing this. You could also talk to a professional dog behaviorist.

P. 84

HOW TO TRAIN YOUR DOG TO GO ON A PUPPY PAD

- Put away any rugs.
- Cover a large area of the floor with puppy pads or newspapers.
- When your dog goes on the pad, praise and reward them!
- If your dog pees on the floor, pat dry the spot with a small piece of newspaper and put it on the pad. This will help the dog to find the right area next time.
- When your dog stops peeing anywhere other than on the pads, you can start slowly taking them away, until there are only two or three left in different spots in the house.

In some cases, an indoor dog potty can be a good alternative. It will not replace going outside for walks, but it can help if you have an older dog that can't hold it as long as they used to, or a small dog that can't handle being outside when it's very cold.

Never scold your dog for peeing inside. Don't rub their nose in their pee or punish them in any other way. This will teach your dog to fear you, and they may hide when they have to "go."

HOW TO TRAIN YOUR DOG TO "GO" OUTSIDE

- Put away all the puppy pads, leaving just one. Clean the house thoroughly to get rid of the smell (you can use a vinegar solution or a special cleaning spray).
- Take the dog outside at regular intervals, around five or six times a day. Slowly increase the amount of time between the intervals—when your dog turns one, you can shorten the number of walks to three a day.
- Set a schedule for feeding and walking your dog. Stick to the schedule! This way, your dog will get used to a predictable daily routine.
- Take your dog outside immediately after they wake up, and after playing, eating, or drinking. Some walks can be long, others can be just short toilet breaks.
- Praise your dog when they go pee or poop outside.
- If your dog continues to have "accidents" inside, wipe those spots clean with vinegar or spray.

Czech researchers have recently found that dogs prefer to align their body along a north-south axis when they do their business. They use Earth's magnetic field to help them position themselves. To find this out, the researchers recorded 1,893 poops and 5,582 pees by seventy dogs over a two-year period.

43

Jo wasn't a small puppy when I first got her, but she kept peeing inside the house for a long time. Imagine a puddle filling about half of the room! I tried everything, followed all the housetraining tips. Took her outside for an hour or longer three times a day, washed the whole apartment to get rid of the smell. Left out a single pad, praised her, and gave her treats every time she went outdoors. I took her to the vet and had some tests done. Nothing worked! For six months, Jo continued to pee indoors…

But one day she suddenly stopped for good, for no apparent reason. I guess it was just the right time. Jo grew up, started to feel more comfortable, and finally figured it all out.

WALKING YOUR DOG

While humans are at school or at work, dogs are sitting around the house all day long, getting bored. They often find ways to deal with this boredom, and that's when we end up with chewed furniture or a great big mess.

On average, adult dogs need to be walked for two hours a day. But it depends on their breed and temperament. An active dog might need longer walks to burn off extra energy. Walks mean not only exercise and running around, they are also a chance to meet other dogs, play games, learn new things, and explore new places. Even tiny toy dogs need new exciting experiences. You don't have to make your sensitive chihuahua spend hours outside in the cold, but you can take them on a walk, drop by a cafe or store, or visit your friends.

Humans have about six million smell receptors in their noses, but dogs have up to 250 million! Their sense of smell is crucial for exploring. On a walk, dogs leave scent markers on trees, bushes, and walls by peeing or pooping. By checking the markers left by other dogs, dogs can tell the gender and age of the dogs who were there before them, whether they're healthy, and even how relaxed or happy they are. When dogs are nervous or aggressive, their hormones create a change in their body scent. So don't be surprised when your dog wants to stop at every other bush. Don't get impatient with them—let them sniff around and explore.

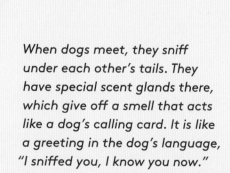

When dogs meet, they sniff under each other's tails. They have special scent glands there, which give off a smell that acts like a dog's calling card. It is like a greeting in the dog's language, "I sniffed you, I know you now."

Clean up your dog's poop! It contains bacteria, worm eggs, or even worms, and it can't be used as a fertilizer. It may make other dogs and people sick.

It is a good idea to try different routes—walking the same path every day for a year will get boring for both the owner and the dog. Some dogs need a change of scenery quite often, others are happy to stick with the same route for a while. Watch your dog—what do they need? Perhaps you could do the same walk during the week and let your dog run in the open fields or in the forest on the weekends. Or do they need a new route every day?

A dog will get tired from an hour-long run in the fields, or from twenty minutes of learning new tricks or playing search games. That's why it's important to alternate between training and games, playing with other dogs, and taking slow walks to explore the landscape. Try to mix it up and make your daily walks more fun.

P. 52

A regular walk
(forty to ninety minutes)
You can do a shorter walk in the morning and a longer one in the evening.

A bathroom break
(ten to fifteen minutes)
You can take the dog out in the middle of the day and before going to sleep, if it's hard for your dog to hold it.

A long walk
Over the weekend, when you have more free time, you can take your dog on longer walks in a park.

HOW MUCH WALKING IS ENOUGH?

Healthy dogs sleep fourteen to eighteen hours a day on average. Large breeds need more time to rest, and young puppies and older dogs also tend to sleep longer. It's perfectly normal that after a good walk your pet will sleep for a good chunk of the day.

If your dog is very active at home, overexcited, and not sleeping much, that means they don't get enough exercise and mental stimulation—not enough to make them tired. They need more walks, playing, and training. It may be the other way around too, if after a long walk, your dog is acting sluggish and apathetic the next day. If they need to recover, let your dog rest in a quiet place, and don't overload them with attention.

Dog harnesses have a long history. The first harnesses were used in Arctic regions for pulling loads on sleds. Some of them date back to around 8,000 years ago.

The leash clips on here.

A harness should be designed to fit the dog's body properly— it shouldn't squeeze the dog's ribcage.

WHY IS A HARNESS BETTER THAN A COLLAR?

We are used to seeing dogs wearing collars but, unfortunately, collars increase the likelihood of an injury. If a dog is energetic or impulsive and pulls on the leash, a collar can damage their windpipe. Dog trainers recommend using a harness, which is safer and kinder. Its straps spread the weight and pressure of the leash away from your dog's neck onto their shoulders, chest, and back. Different types of harnesses are used for different purposes: weight pulling, sledding, training, harnesses for guide dogs, search and rescue, and other kinds of working dogs. You will need one designed for walking. It's important to pick the right style of harness for your dog.

ON-LEASH VS OFF-LEASH?

Always keep your dog on a leash in public areas. At parks, check the local rules to see if letting your dog off the leash is allowed.

Don't let your dog off the leash unless they reliably come to you when called. If they ignore your commands, it's better not to risk it. Your pet can easily run away and get lost. It's also kind to think about other people who may not like dogs as much as you do!

It is a good idea to have two leashes: a short one (five to seven feet) for short walks and rides on public transit, and a longer one (fifteen to twenty feet) that gives your dog more freedom. With a longer leash, you can train your dog outdoors and not worry about them running away.

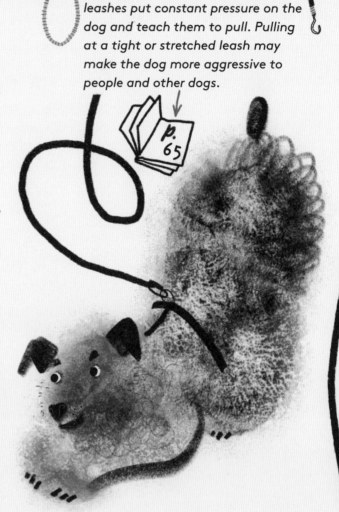

Why a fixed-length leash instead of a retractable leash? Retractable leashes put constant pressure on the dog and teach them to pull. Pulling at a tight or stretched leash may make the dog more aggressive to people and other dogs.

p. 65

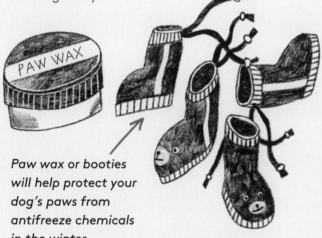

Paw wax or booties will help protect your dog's paws from antifreeze chemicals in the winter.

If you have a short-haired dog that's sensitive to cold, dress them according to the weather.

Clean your dog's paws after every walk. You will need a bucket or a large bowl of water and towels to dry their wet feet. If you have a small dog, you can give their paws a rinse in a sink. And if your dog is covered with dirt from nose to tail, a bathtub is the way to go. From the start, teach your puppy to let you wipe their paws. They need to learn to wait calmly while you get ready to wash them.

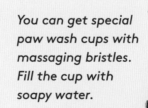

You can get special paw wash cups with massaging bristles. Fill the cup with soapy water.

We live close to the center of Moscow, but it is nice to take walks in our neighborhood. There is a river nearby and a small park where Jo and I go to watch the boats and the water rushing through the floodgates. Sometimes we just walk around—go to an old Soviet grocery store to get some bread and milk, or cross the river and walk into a small gated park. Occasionally, we see woodpeckers and squirrels there. If we go early in the morning, and there is no one else around, I take Jo off the leash and play ball with her. It's especially nice there in the autumn when the ground is covered with yellow and red maple leaves and Jo runs through them, chest-deep.

But what we love most of all is leaving the city to visit my parents. They have their own house and there's a forest, a river, and a field nearby—that's the life! Jo runs around in the grass, digs holes, hunts for mice, and splashes in the river. Every time we visit, it's hard to go back to the city.

GAMES AND ENRICHMENT

Dogs love to play! Puppies play most of the time... well, okay, most of the time they sleep. But they do play a lot as a way of learning about the world. Games are as important as walks, even for an adult dog. Play is vital for creating a bond with your pet. It can also be used as an effective way to train your dog.

There are different kinds of games: physical activities that tire your dog out, and enrichment games that require a lot of thinking, which is tiring in a different way. Many city dogs don't get enough exercise, so brain stimulation can help make up for that.

One of the smartest dogs in the world was Chaser, a border collie. Her owner, the psychologist John W. Pilley, taught her 1,022 words by showing her different objects and repeating their names. Chaser had about 800 stuffed toys, 116 balls, twenty-six frisbees, and lots of plastic toys, and could identify all of them by name.

ACTIVE GAMES

CHASE

Run with your dog. Chase them and let them chase you.

FETCH

Throw a ball and have your pet bring it back to you. Some dogs don't like to let go of the ball. Don't chase the dog and don't try to take the ball. Praise and give treats to encourage your dog to drop it.

HIDE AND SEEK

This game improves visual contact with your dog. Start playing indoors, hiding behind a chair or a couch. Praise your dog when they find you. Then you can move on to playing outdoors. Try hiding behind a tree or a bush. This game can be dangerous for fearful or young dogs, so make sure it's appropriate for your pet.

TUG OF WAR

Many dogs love to play tug. Just remember to follow a few rules to play it safely: start and end the game on your command (for example, "get it" and "drop it"). The game stops if your dog's teeth touch your skin.

BRAIN GAMES

Most brain games for dogs involve searching for food and eventually finding it. Your dog will get lots of satisfaction from doing this and will feel more confident. Start with simple games. Help your dog if they're struggling!

Kibble, pieces of boiled chicken or beef, liver bites

The easiest game! Hide a treat in one of your hands. Let your dog sniff and guess which hand the treat is hiding in. Start with treats that have a strong scent.

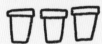

You can play the same game with paper cups.

ROLL UP

Place treats over the whole area of a towel and roll it up. The dog will have to figure out how to unravel it.

BOX GAME

Roll treats up in small pieces of paper and put them into a cardboard box. Leave some of the crumpled up papers empty.

BOTTLE GAME

Kibble inside

Hole in the middle of the bottle

Put treats inside a bottle and tape it up. For a more advanced version, roll the treats up in paper and screw the bottle cap back on.

SNUFFLE MAT

This is a great way to keep a dog busy for a while. If your pet finds and eats food too fast, you could serve daily meals on this mat.

Fleece strips

Supervise your dog while they play these games. If they like to eat paper or plastic, avoid games that use those materials.

Rubber mat with holes (door mat, sink or shower mat).

Push each strip through the hole and tie a double knot.

Hide treats among the fleece strips and tell your dog to "find it."

INTERACTIVE TOYS

You can also get special interactive puzzle and chew toys. These provide mental stimulation and enrichment, satisfying the dog's instinctive need to find food and to chew. These toys are filled with treats (see below for things to put inside). The goal is for the dog to get to the treats. You can make it harder or easier for the dog, depending on the type of the toy and consistency of the treats. For instance, to make it more challenging, freeze the entire toy.

KONG is one of the most popular toys of this kind. It was invented in the 1970s. Joe Markham noticed that his three-year-old German shepherd Fritz loved to chew rocks and his teeth were starting to wear down. He would destroy store-bought toys in seconds. One day, Joe was fixing his car and Fritz started chewing on a strangely shaped rubber shock absorber. This inspired Markham to create the KONG dog toy.

TOY STUFFING RECIPES

1. Slice fruit into small pieces. Any kind will do, as long as your dog is not allergic. Bananas can be pureed. Mix all ingredients together, add organic yogurt. Put the mixture inside the toy and freeze for three to four hours.

The original car part looked like this. The toy is almost exactly the same shape.

Seal the small hole with something thick (peanut butter, cream cheese, pieces of canned food) and put treats inside.

The treats could be kibble, small pieces of vegetables, or dog biscuits.

2. Cut cheese into cubes, crumble up dog biscuits, mix with farmer's cheese. You can freeze this mixture or use it as it is.

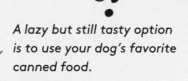

A lazy but still tasty option is to use your dog's favorite canned food.

3. Chop raw or boiled meat into cubes, mix with cooked rice and raw or boiled carrots (grate or dice them too).

ANTLERS

Reindeer antlers are considered to be one of the best chew treats. They have no smell and are made up of mainly calcium and phosphorus. They also include many other minerals and amino acids. Choose only soft antlers.

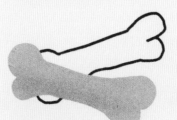

BONES

Bones can be pretty dangerous for dogs: poultry and pork bones can injure the inside of your dog's mouth and stomach, and cooked bones can cause intestinal blockages. It is relatively safe to give beef knuckle, marrow, or lamb tail bones. Important: Only give raw meat bones!

EARS AND TAILS

You can get a variety of dried chew treats at the supermarket (pig ears, cow hooves and tails, etc.). These do not replace bones or antlers because they are not as hard, but they work well as extra treats.

WHY DO DOGS LIKE TO CHEW?

When dogs move their jaws to chew, their body produces a chemical called acetylcholine, which has a relaxing effect. It's like meditation for dogs. If a dog gets stressed or scared, chewing on something is a way to calm down. The same thing will happen if a dog doesn't get enough physical exercise or mental stimulation. Chewing is a perfectly normal activity—just make sure your shoes are safely out of the way! It's a good idea to offer chew toys and edible chew treats to prevent any destructive chewing.

Chewing is also how dogs keep their jaws strong and their teeth healthy!

Jo destroyed a ton of stuff, mostly during her teenage phase. She stopped when she was a year and a half. But she did have a lot of fun! Try counting how many things she's chewed.

HOW TO TRAIN YOUR DOG

For a long time, dominance theory was a widely used method of dog training. Dog owners were told to show the dog who's boss and be the "alpha." Rules included not allowing the dog to go through doorways first, eat first, or climb on their owner's bed. They also involved aggressive behavior toward the dog, including force and physical punishment. Modern dog training no longer relies on this kind of dominance. Instead, the best approach is to use positive reinforcement. What is that?

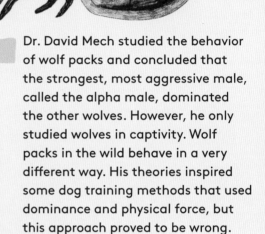

Dr. David Mech studied the behavior of wolf packs and concluded that the strongest, most aggressive male, called the alpha male, dominated the other wolves. However, he only studied wolves in captivity. Wolf packs in the wild behave in a very different way. His theories inspired some dog training methods that used dominance and physical force, but this approach proved to be wrong.

Don't hit or threaten your dog when they behave badly. This will damage your relationship with them.

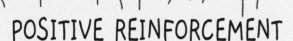

POSITIVE REINFORCEMENT

Using positive reinforcement to train your dog means you reward the behaviors you want and ignore the behaviors you don't want. The reward makes the dog more likely to repeat the good behavior. As well as correcting bad behavior, positive reinforcement is a good way to teach your dog pretty much anything, from basic commands to difficult tricks. Dogs love to work and get rewarded. They think, "Ah, if I do this now, I'll get a tasty treat!" And the best and most important thing is that this improves your bond with your dog.

Pinch collars, which have sharp prongs, and e-collars, which deliver an electric shock, are cruel and harmful to dogs. Never use them!

HOW TO REWARD YOUR DOG

- Treats work especially well! Give your dog a treat as soon as they do something right. Do it every time at first. Once they have reliably learned the behavior, you can switch to giving treats occasionally. This is called continuous reinforcement.
- Praise. Use verbal rewards. Say something like "yes!" or "good dog!" in an enthusiastic tone of voice. Then give your dog a treat.
- Marker word or clicker (optional). As soon as your dog demonstrates the desired behavior, click the clicker or say the marker word and give a treat. The marker can be any word you like ("yes!", "good dog!", "great!"). Your dog will associate the sound of a clicker or the marker word with getting a treat and will know that they're doing the right thing.

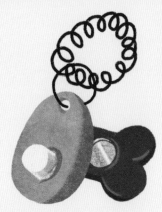

A clicker is a simple device that makes a "click" sound when you press the button. There are various styles and shapes on sale. Many come with a wrist band you can wear.

Start training at home to minimize distractions.

Outside, find a quiet place where your dog will not be distracted by other people, dogs or cars.

When your dog can immediately respond to your commands in a quiet spot, you can move on to a more crowded place.

CHOOSING TREATS

- A treat should be something your pet really loves.
- It should be a very small (pea-sized or smaller), soft piece of food. Your dog should be able to immediately gulp it down. Make sure your dog doesn't overeat throughout the day.
- Carry enough treats so that you don't run out at the wrong time! For example, bring eighty to one hundred treats for one training session. Count those calories as part of your dog's daily food intake.
- A treat should be healthy and low in fat. What could that be? Small pieces of boiled chicken, beef, liver, dog biscuits—even pieces of cheese or sausage on rare occasions (these are not very healthy foods for dogs).

When going outside, it's better to keep dog treats in a pocket or a belt bag where you can reach them easily, sealed in a plastic bag.

You can train your dog yourself, or you can take a basic obedience training class. It's like an elementary school for dogs. You can even find a training boot camp, where you leave your pet for up to a month and then get a perfectly well-behaved dog at the end of the stay. I don't recommend doing that, however. Ideally, owners should train their own dogs, either at home or in a group class. Training helps with bonding and your dog's development. They have to constantly think and learn new things. Once your dog knows basic obedience commands, you can move on to teaching them tricks. You could teach your dog to shake paws, bring you your slippers, open a door, or even dance!

Here are a few basic commands to teach your dog:

> There is a dog sport called agility, in which a handler guides a dog around an obstacle course. Points are given for speed and precision. This sport first appeared in the 1970s in the U.K.

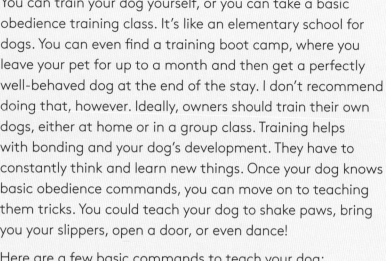

Never punish your dog for coming to you—even if they run away and you can't catch them. You want your dog to associate the "come" command with good things.

COME

- This is the most important and most complicated command to master. Until you can reliably recall your dog, you can only let your dog run off-leash in fenced-in places.
- Show your dog a treat.
- Call your dog to come. Don't repeat yourself.
- When the dog comes to you, give them lots of praise, then reward them.

SIT

- Show your dog a treat. Put it right in front of their nose.
- Say "sit."
- Lift the treat above the dog's head so that they will sit as they lift their head to nibble at the treat.
- Allow them to eat the treat and praise when their bottom touches the ground.

DOWN

- Show your dog a treat.
- Say "down."
- Slowly bring the treat to the floor. If the dog doesn't lie down, hold the treat in your fist on the floor, luring the dog to try to get it.
- Let them eat the treat and give lots of praise when they lie down.

HEEL

- Showing a treat, guide your dog to stand next to your leg.
- Hold the treat in your hand by your leg, so the dog will try to nibble the treat.
- Take a few steps forward and stop. If the dog runs in front of you, wait until they come back. Reward them in place.
- Continue moving forward and stopping. When your dog learns to walk at your side, you can make things harder: walk in a semicircle or zigzag pattern, change direction, etc.

A well-trained dog and a well-behaved dog are not the same thing. A dog can know and obey a lot of commands, but still behave badly. A dog is well-behaved when you can comfortably and happily live together. To get there, never stop training your dog.

Picture this. Your dog is next to the dinner table, whining for food. You give in and share a small piece. Aha! It works! Next time, they will whine more to get something yummy. If you don't mind sharing a piece of food, it's better to wait until your dog calmly sits down and asks for it. It's also important to remember that rewarding does not necessarily mean giving treats. For example, when you come back home at the end of a long day, your dog may be so happy to see you that they don't let you take your coat off. If you try to calm them down first, the dog is rewarded with your attention—exactly what they want! It would be better to wait until they calm down themselves. Then you can pet your dog and say hello.

- **Never force your dog to do or not do something.**
- **Training should be fun for you and your dog.**
- **Pay attention to your dog. If they are tired and find it hard to concentrate, take a break or stop training for the day.**

Jo knows a lot! She is no circus dog, of course, but she knows a lot of commands. But what I'm most proud of is our bond. Even when we're out in the fields, with Jo running free as the wind, every two or three minutes she'll check for me. She turns her head, looks at me, and runs over. That makes me so happy. I always pet her and give her a gentle hug.

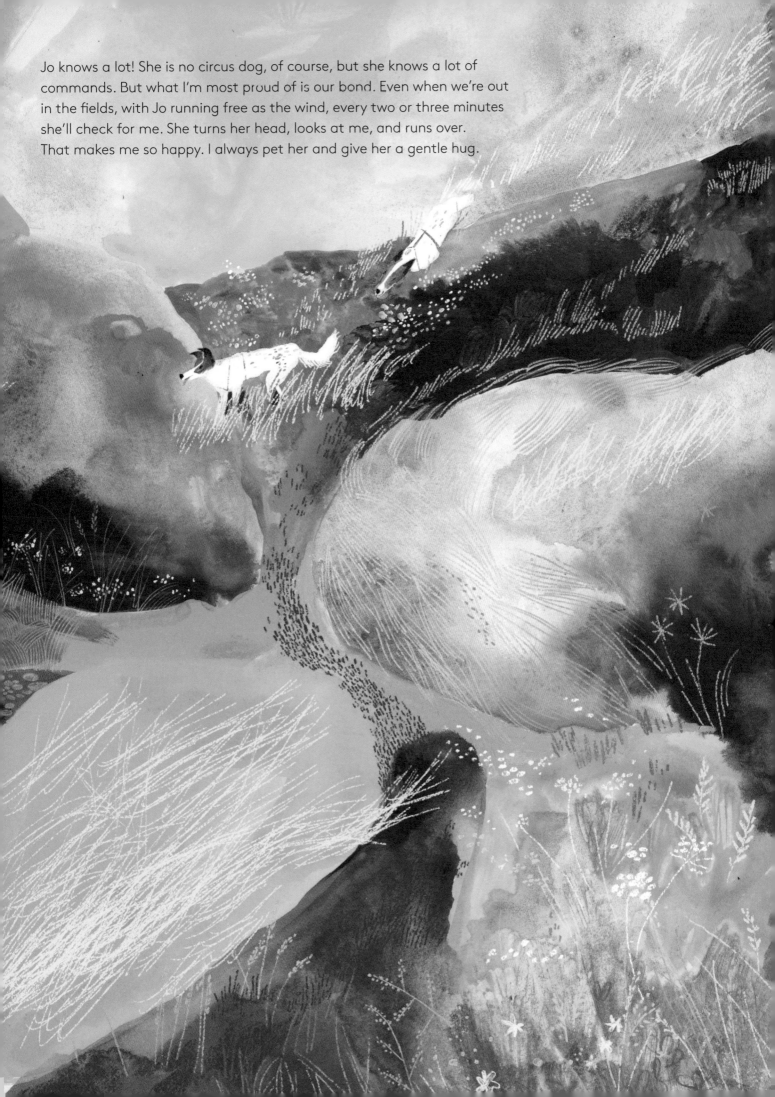

YOUR DOG AND OTHER DOGS

Puppies are usually happy to meet other dogs—they are friendly and often excited to make new friends and play. But as dogs get older, their behavior may change. Some dogs stay friendly with everyone, some become aggressive with unfamiliar dogs, and others remain faithful to their old friends but lose interest in all other dogs. In any case, socializing with their own kind is very important for a dog's wellbeing. Animals use body language to communicate with each other. An isolated dog will not learn these crucial skills. Dogs communicate by using facial expressions and body postures, which can range from very subtle to clear and obvious.

When dogs want to avoid conflict, they use calming signals. They can use them with other dogs and with humans too.

There are at least thirty calming signals. Dogs might turn their head to the side and look away, or turn completely around showing their back; they might lick their lips, yawn, sit down or lie down when they see another dog, sniff the ground, or start moving slowly. They may also walk in a curve when approaching other dogs.

"Calming signals" is a term invented by Norwegian dog trainer Turid Rugaas in the 1990s. She and her team spent many years watching and recording how dogs communicate with each other.

When interacting with your dog, watch for body language clues. Does your dog want to communicate with you or not?

64

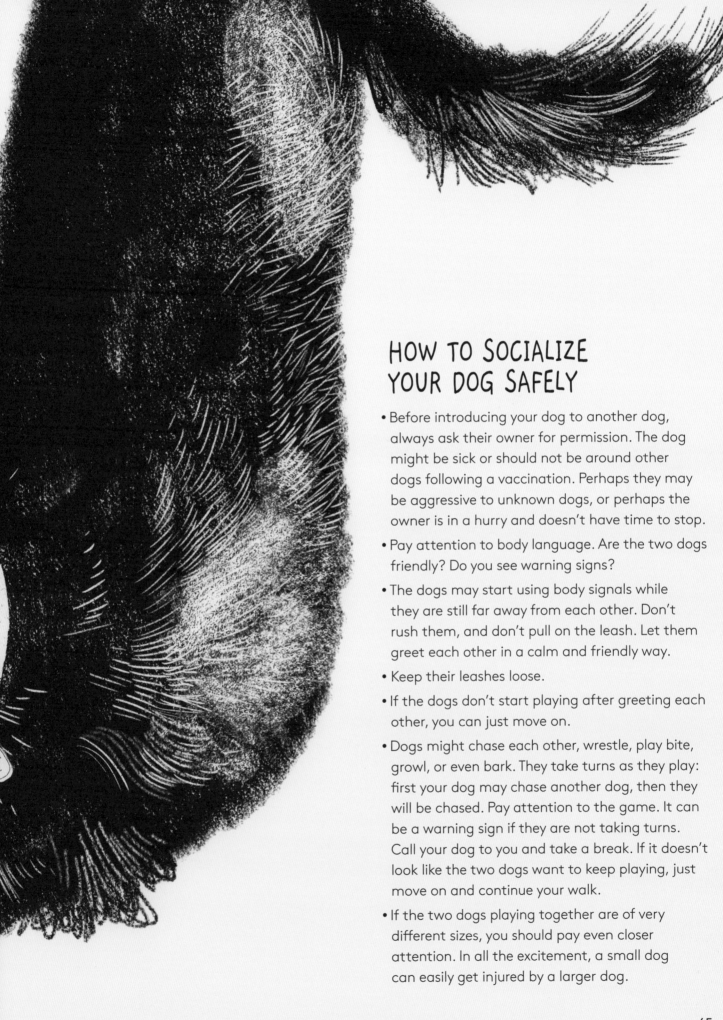

HOW TO SOCIALIZE YOUR DOG SAFELY

- Before introducing your dog to another dog, always ask their owner for permission. The dog might be sick or should not be around other dogs following a vaccination. Perhaps they may be aggressive to unknown dogs, or perhaps the owner is in a hurry and doesn't have time to stop.

- Pay attention to body language. Are the two dogs friendly? Do you see warning signs?

- The dogs may start using body signals while they are still far away from each other. Don't rush them, and don't pull on the leash. Let them greet each other in a calm and friendly way.

- Keep their leashes loose.

- If the dogs don't start playing after greeting each other, you can just move on.

- Dogs might chase each other, wrestle, play bite, growl, or even bark. They take turns as they play: first your dog may chase another dog, then they will be chased. Pay attention to the game. It can be a warning sign if they are not taking turns. Call your dog to you and take a break. If it doesn't look like the two dogs want to keep playing, just move on and continue your walk.

- If the two dogs playing together are of very different sizes, you should pay even closer attention. In all the excitement, a small dog can easily get injured by a larger dog.

Jo is a very friendly dog. She loves everybody: children, adults, other dogs, and even cats! And everyone loves her back—except maybe cats, that is. Once Jo stopped being afraid of the street, our walks became very exciting. I'd been living in my apartment for a year before I got Jo, and didn't know anyone but my closest neighbors. With Jo, I got to know everyone in our courtyard and almost every dog owner in the neighborhood.

All the local children between two and five years old absolutely adore Jo. On dark winter nights, she plays ball with the kids on the playground. She has a best friend called Cinnamon, a brown dog with an olive-colored nose. She is a mixed-breed dog like Jo, but her owners call her an Australian Olive Shepherd, just for fun. She is a real beauty!

DOG GROOMING

A CLEAN COAT

Bathe your dog as frequently as you need to. If a dog's coat looks greasy, smells bad, or got covered in mud—it's time for a bath. It's probably best to leave more advanced grooming to a professional. Dog groomers can do haircuts, hand stripping (removing dead hairs from the coat for wiry haired dogs), and can even trim your dog's nails.

Brush your dog's coat regularly. How often you need to do it depends on hair length and whether your dog is shedding or not. Brushing removes excess hair, stimulates new skin cell production, encourages hair growth, and cuts down on the amount of hair you have to deal with on your furniture and rugs!

Examine your dog regularly. Make it fun. While petting your dog or giving them a massage, check for any bites, rashes, scratches, lumps, or bumps.

Use a special dog shampoo that won't damage the dog's skin and coat.

Go easy with hairdryers, although they're sometimes necessary for long-haired dogs. Set the dryer to the lowest heat setting and keep the nozzle a few inches away from your dog's fur. Short-haired dogs can be rubbed with a towel and left to dry on their own.

The quick is visible on paler dog nails. On dark nails it's not always easy to see.

Clip here

NEAT NAILS

Some dogs naturally wear down their nails from frequent walks on city streets. But if they don't, they will need to have their nails trimmed. Clip only the tip of the nail, not hitting the "quick," a blood vessel that runs into the nail. A nick there is painful and will bleed.

TOP-NOTCH TEETH

When plaque collects on teeth, it can harden into tartar. Check your dog's teeth regularly. Plaque can be easily removed by cleaning your dog's teeth at home, but a large build-up of tartar will require professional cleaning.

Dogs have forty-two teeth—twenty on top and twenty-two on the bottom.

To stop plaque from building up, brush your dog's teeth with a special dog toothbrush and dog toothpaste.

If you do hit the quick, apply some styptic powder or corn starch to stop the bleeding.

If your dog is too afraid to have their nails trimmed, you can try a nail grinder—an electric tool that sands nails down.

Give your dog treats during and after grooming. That way, you'll create a positive association for something that might not always be pleasant.

Oh boy, Jo sheds a lot! Her hair gets everywhere: on the floor, on the couch, on my clothes and sometimes even in my food! It feels like Jo sheds not just twice a year, but constantly. I've tried changing her diet, giving her vitamins, and talked to vets. But vets say that Jo probably has a special gene from her ancestors that makes her shed all the time. I don't know if it's true or not, but a vacuum cleaner has become my best friend—along with lint rollers and a tolerant attitude.

VISITING THE VET

Just like us, dogs can get sick. Many dogs are afraid or unhappy about seeing the vet because they associate it with unpleasant things—there is often plenty of poking and prodding, and this may be painful. But going to the vet is essential to a dog's long-term health. These visits can be for regular check-ups, vaccinations, treatment for chronic diseases, accidents, or unexpected issues: dogs can get food poisoning or get injured, they may get an infection, or be bitten by a tick or another dog.

To ease the stress and anxiety of vet visits, get your dog used to the vet at an early stage. Find a good vet clinic, ideally, not too far from home, and take your dog for a visit, just to look around. Let your dog sniff and explore the place, give them a yummy treat, then continue with your regular walk. Repeat this a few times until your dog gets comfortable with the clinic and possibly starts to associate the place with something exciting. That way, vet visits will be a much more pleasant experience.

This is an inpatient ward for sick pets that require longer monitoring and treatment.

And this is an ultrasound room.

This is a reception area, where owners wait with their pets.

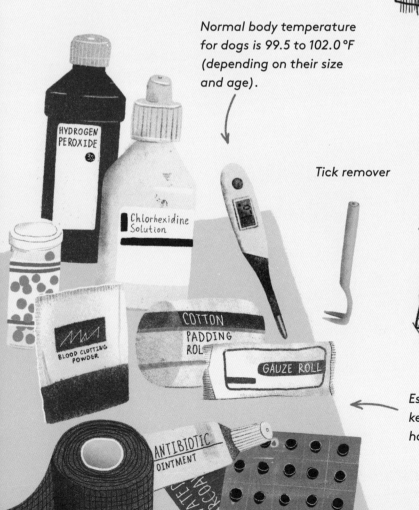

Normal body temperature for dogs is 99.5 to 102.0 °F (depending on their size and age).

HYDROGEN PEROXIDE

Chlorhexidine Solution

Tick remover

BLOOD CLOTTING POWDER

COTTON PADDING ROL

GAUZE ROLL

ANTIBIOTIC OINTMENT

Essential items to keep in your dog's home first aid kit.

This is a treatment room.

Ticks often hide in tall grasses and weeds, so getting a tick is more likely in a forest or in the open countryside. But they can also be found in city parks.

This tiny spider-like creature can be deadly for dogs. It is a sheep tick. Ticks can carry a disease called babesiosis. Without timely diagnosis and medical treatment, a dog will die within a week from the time of the tick bite. It is most common in southern U.S. states.

Check your pet after every walk during peak tick season (March to November, or year-round in some places). Consider using special tick prevention products. There are drops, pills, collars, and tick repellents available. Pills are often the most effective option. Talk to your vet about the best products to protect your dog against ticks.

Here is an exam room.

Here is an operating room.

Keep up with your dog's vaccination schedule.
Deworm your dog regularly.
Take your dog to the vet for routine checkups.
You can give first aid to your dog in an emergency, but always contact your vet too.

Jo and I are regular visitors to the vet's clinic: routine vaccinations, cut paw pads, nose scratched by a cat. But the scariest thing happened last spring: Jo had a tick. I noticed that she had become drowsy and weak and her temperature was very high. Jo had contracted babesiosis. For a week, nobody knew if she would survive. It took about a month of medical treatment before she got better. I was so happy when she was able to eat again and wag her tail a little!

How often does your family go on vacation? Are you able to take your dog with you or can you leave them with your friends or relatives? You might have to pay for a boarding kennel, where professional staff will take care of your dog while your family is away.

Even if you don't do any long-distance travel, sometimes you have to take your dog on public transit or in a car with you—to go to a park, visit your friends, or go hiking. To make sure the experience is pleasant and stress-free, start getting your dog used to transit while they're still young.

There are different guidelines and safety rules for dog travel on different types of transit.

If you're traveling overseas with your dog, you will need special documents, depending on where you live and where you're going to. Make sure you check the rules before you travel!

> Never leave your dog alone in a car! Even on a cool day, a car can get dangerously hot in the sun, putting your dog at risk of heatstroke.

BY CAR

Dogs must not move around inside the car. For a smaller dog, you can use a travel crate. A larger dog will be safer and more comfortable in a back-seat hammock, with an installed back-seat barrier or a dog guard in the trunk.

ON PUBLIC TRANSIT

Check the rules for buses, trams, or subway trains where you live because they can vary a lot. In some places, dogs must be kept in carriers. In other places, dogs are allowed but cannot travel at peak times.

BY PLANE

Some airlines let small dogs in the cabin, if they are in a carrier, but many only allow service dogs to travel in the cabin. Other dogs must travel in crates in the luggage compartment. Rules vary from airline to airline, so you should check the regulations well in advance.

Flying is very stressful for dogs. Talk to your vet about whether your dog should be given a sedative for travel.

BY TRAIN

The rules for taking dogs on trains vary according to where you live. In the U.S. only small dogs are allowed and must travel inside a secure carrier. In some countries, you may need to buy your dog a special ticket, or may only be able to travel in one particular car of the train.

ON THE SUBWAY

You are allowed to take your dog on most U.S. subway trains but only if they are carried in a secure container and do not disturb other passengers. Service dogs are also permitted.

I often ride trains with Jo, and every time it's a real adventure. Everyone gives her attention—children, grandmas, men with hunting stories, and all kinds of other people. I remember one day in particular.

It is late spring or early summer. I'm wearing a new dress with a ragged hem, my favorite brightly colored sneakers, a huge backpack, and a fanny pack. Fresh and glowing, I'm on the train with Jo, going to spend the weekend in the country. Jo is wearing a stylish collar, a harness, and a matching muzzle. Just look at this white, shiny, and incredibly beautiful dog! I'm having a chat with a woman and her young daughter, who is very interested in Jo.

We've been riding for an hour. It's hot—I take out Jo's bowl and pour some water. She drinks the water, but there's still some left. We are about to arrive at our station, so we start heading for the exit. I still have the bowl in my hands—we're going to get off the train in a moment and I'll dump the rest of the water under a bush. The woman and her daughter follow us into the train corridor. Jo is standing there, waiting for the train to stop. I'm loaded down with bags, clasping the bowl to my chest. And the woman... throws some money into the bowl and says, "I never give money to people on the street, but that doggie is just too cute!"

IF YOUR DOG IS SCARED

Every dog is different. Some dogs are always confident, but others are anxious and easily scared. Dogs can be afraid of lots of things: noises, people, other dogs, cars, or buses—in fact, almost anything, however silly it may seem. Some fears are the result of bad experiences. For instance, if a neighbor with a beard used to scare your puppy away from his gate, your adult dog might become afraid of all bearded men. Other fears are common among dogs, like fear of thunderstorms or fireworks.

How do you help a fearful dog? Help your dog feel safe by having a predictable schedule and routine. Boost your dog's confidence: work on their training, give them plenty of praise and rewards. It is possible to overcome some fears, but others you will just to have to deal with. Sometimes the only option is to avoid the things that scare your dog.

One of the main techniques used to help dogs overcome their fears is called counterconditioning. For example, you might show your dog a thing that scares them, at a distance at first, and give your dog a delicious treat. Over time, you would gradually shorten the distance. Your dog will learn to associate this thing with yummy food, and so they will learn to like it. Just be sure to go very slowly. Rushing will only make fear worse. If your dog has a very strong fear reaction, talk to a professional dog behaviorist.

Don't shout at your dog when they're scared. Accept their fear, pet them, and talk to them in a soothing voice. Don't just ignore the fear, but also don't go overboard with consoling—your dog might think something scary really IS going on and this may reinforce the behavior.

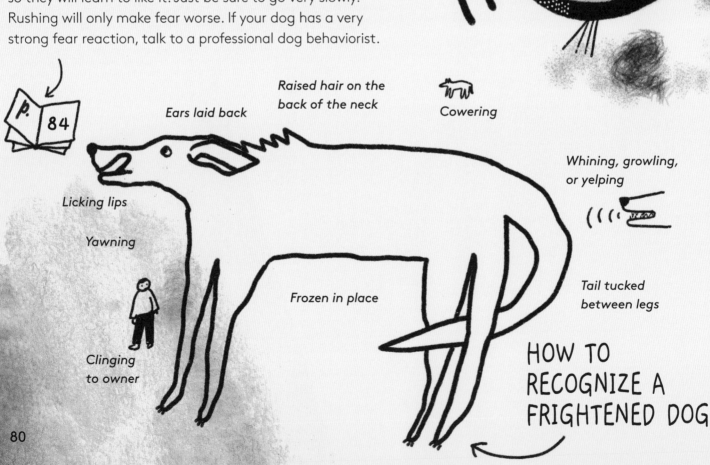

p. 84

Ears laid back

Raised hair on the back of the neck

Cowering

Licking lips

Yawning

Whining, growling, or yelping

Frozen in place

Tail tucked between legs

Clinging to owner

HOW TO RECOGNIZE A FRIGHTENED DOG

Dogs have much more sensitive ears than humans. We can detect sounds in a frequency range from about 20 to 20,000 Hz. Dogs have a wider range—from 12 to 65,000 Hz. In fact, dogs can hear sounds almost a mile away! That means they are more sensitive to noises—loud sounds can even cause them pain!

FIREWORKS

The loud booming of fireworks in the sky often frightens dogs. Sometimes they can get loose or slip out of their collars and run off in a panic.

- Dogs should always wear collars with ID tags.
- Keep your dog on a leash.
- Change your walking routine for the day. Do the main long walk in the morning, another walk during the day, if possible, and just a quick five-minute bathroom break at night.
- Antianxiety medication might help, but always talk to your vet first.

THUNDERSTORMS

Dogs can sense when a storm is approaching. Storms come not only with the loud rumbling of thunder, but also with a rapid change of air pressure and high levels of static electricity.

- Check the weather forecast for thunderstorms. Make sure to take your dog out for a good, long walk before the storm.
- Give your dog a safe place to go during a storm.
- Play loud music or turn the volume on the TV up high to help cancel out the sound of the storm.
- Distract your dog from the noise by giving them attention—play with them, talk to them, give them something tasty to eat.
- You could try training your dog to get used to the sounds by playing a recording of thunder, gradually increasing the volume and always pairing it with positive distractions: playing, training, giving treats or toys. However, this may not always work.

Jo is great with riding cars and okay with riding trains (although she doesn't like it much). But she thinks that city trams are the scariest monsters in the world! They rumble and rattle, they clang and squeal, they spit smoke and fire. From a dog's point of view, they're dragons!

Whenever we see a tram, Jo darts past it at full speed, her ears laid back, knocking down everything in her path. All I can do is try to hold on to the other end of the leash.

I'm still trying to work on this fear of hers and have talked to dog trainers, but with no success yet.
We might have to start avoiding trams altogether.

WHEN YOUR DOG BEHAVES BADLY

Peeing and pooping indoors

Aggression

Fears and phobias

Howling and barking when left alone

A dog trainer may provide basic obedience training, or special training for other activities. They don't usually deal with problem behavior in dogs.

Eating food off the street

When we imagine getting a dog, we usually picture a perfect pet—obedient, calm, and quick to understand us. Of course, there are a few dogs like that, but dogs usually need lots of time and training before they can do everything we want.

Most dogs are a long way from perfect. However, some things that humans see as problems—chewing, digging, barking, rolling in dirt—are perfectly normal for dogs. We should always keep that in mind.

However, there are behavior problems that can greatly affect both our lives and our pet's: aggression toward people or other dogs, peeing and pooping indoors, fears and phobias of various kinds (separation anxiety, fear of loud noises, fear of certain objects), hyperactivity, destructive chewing, eating things off the streets. Solving these doggy problems requires dedication and hard work.

Destructive chewing

WHAT CAN YOU DO?

Get your dog examined by a vet. Behavior problems are often caused by an underlying health issue. For example, if your dog has suddenly started to pee in the house or is acting aggressively, they may be in pain.

If your dog is healthy overall, you can try solving behavior problems on your own. There are lots of resources available, including guidelines for addressing common dog issues.

p. 94

If you can't solve the problem on your own, you'll need to speak to a dog behaviorist.

A dog behaviorist is a specially trained expert. Their job is to help you manage, change, or prevent problem behavior in dogs.

When looking for a dog behaviorist, find someone with professional training and good recommendations, and think about the methods they use (force-free training, no choke collars). A good behaviorist works with the dog owner and helps them get the most out of their relationship with their pet.

Hyperactivity

Jo is a fearful dog by nature, and nobody knows what her life was like when she was a puppy. That's why she will never be very brave or self-assured. Her main problems are also connected with her fears. She is afraid of trams and starts to frantically pull on the leash. She is also afraid of having her claws trimmed and hides whenever she sees me with the clippers. But I accept her the way she is.

Jo is a wonderful dog. She is sweet, affectionate, and loves everybody. And when we are together, we can handle anything!

WHEN DOGS GET OLDER

Until recently, the longest living dog of all time was an Australian cattle dog named Bluey (1910-1939). Bluey lived twenty-nine years and five months.

In 2023, Guinness World Records announced that a new record holder had been found. The oldest dog ever recorded is now Bobi, a Rafeiro do Alentejo from Portugal, who was thirty years and seven months old in February 2023.

Dogs grow up at different speeds. Small dogs are fully grown by the age of twelve months, while larger breeds can still be considered puppies for a year and a half or even two years. But a dog's life is shorter than a human's. An adorable little puppy quickly grows into an active, curious teenager, and then into a confident adult dog. In just a few years, they will slowly start to age.

Dogs live an average of ten to fourteen years. Their lifespan varies according to their adult size and breed. Toy dogs grow up faster but live longer. Smaller dogs typically live fourteen to seventeen years, and some huge dog breeds such as Great Danes live only eight to ten years. That is why dogs age at different rates.

SIGNS YOUR DOG IS AGING

- Changes in behavior. Your high-energy dog may sleep more during the day. They may also start avoiding other dogs.
- Your dog may become grumpy and might snap or growl if they don't like something.
- Loss of sight, hearing, or smell. Your dog may ignore your commands because they can't hear you.
- Tooth decay and gum infections.
- Graying fur or a coat that becomes dull or thin.

People sometimes say that one dog year is equal to seven human years. This is not true, however, because different dog breeds have different lifespans.

CARING FOR AN OLDER DOG

- Visit your vet for regular check-ups. This will help spot health problems early. If a problem can't be treated, the vet will help to keep it under control.

- Make sure your dog gets enough regular exercise and mental stimulation. Look for new routes for regular walks, continue to train your dog, teach them tricks, or play enrichment games.

- Feed your dog a healthy diet so that their body weight stays steady.

- Keep to your usual daily routine. If your dog's day is unpredictable, it can lead to increased levels of stress.

Enjoy every moment with your dog—they won't be around forever. Go for lots of walks, play, and have fun together.

When Jo was little, she was a goofball. She'd often get her leash in a tangle or wildly pull toward every dog or child we'd meet. She also ignored most of my commands, and I'd think, "What a silly dog I have!" But then Jo grew bigger, and all of a sudden, she got smarter. I now live with a dog that understands almost every word I say, and sometimes she understands me even without words. Talk to your dog! The more you talk to them, the more they will understand.

THE FIVE FREEDOMS

What are the Five Freedoms? The Five Freedoms are internationally accepted standards of care that state every animal's right to humane treatment—including dogs, of course. Developed in 1965 and formalized in 1979, they represent the minimum standards of care that owners should provide for their dogs to keep them healthy and happy. Most dog behavior problems happen when these conditions are not met.

In 1822, thanks to a politician named Richard Martin, the British Parliament passed a law preventing cruelty to animals. Martin campaigned for animal rights on streets of London, and became the target of jokes and cartoons that showed him with donkey ears.

FREEDOM FROM HUNGER AND THIRST

Your dog should have easy access to fresh water and food to keep them healthy.

FREEDOM FROM DISCOMFORT

You should provide an appropriate environment including shelter and a comfortable resting area.

FREEDOM FROM PAIN, INJURY, OR DISEASE

Your dog should have access to necessary health check-ups and medical treatment. They should not suffer from pain.

FREEDOM TO EXPRESS NORMAL BEHAVIOR

Dogs need to be able to interact with others of their own kind when they want to. They must be able to run, jump, and play together, sniff, dig, and bark!

FREEDOM FROM FEAR AND DISTRESS

Never scare or hurt your dog on purpose. They should not feel stressed or bored. Give them enough enrichment and use only humane methods of dog training.

First, make sure you really want a dog.
Before you get one, think carefully and decide
if your family is ready for this responsibility.

Remember that a dog is not a toy. They are living
creatures, with their own personality and habits.
Owning a dog takes a lot of time and commitment.
Be prepared before you bring a dog into your family.
Be patient, don't rush your dog, and don't get upset
if some things don't work out right away. Watch your
dog, learn about their personality, and work out what
they like and don't like. Train your dog and provide
enrichment. Enjoy the time you spend together. Don't
scold your dog for mishaps and don't hurt them. Try
to understand what might be causing any unwanted
behavior and find ways to prevent it.

If you need help to tackle your dog's issues, talk to a
specialist—a vet, a dog trainer, or a dog behaviorist.
Learn more by reading professional dog training
books and blogs.

Most importantly, love your dog and try to be their
best friend. Dogs are absolutely amazing. They bring
us joy and make us happy. And your dog is the best!

ACKNOWLEDGMENTS AND USEFUL RESOURCES

THE FOLLOWING EXPERTS CONTRIBUTED TO THIS BOOK:

BATLAY

ANTON VOLKOV

Dog behaviorist
volkovosobakah.pro
🅾 volkov_osobakah

BAGEL

KATYA BAKRO

Social activist
and dog lover

CHENYA

PAVEL TOCHILOVSKIY

Veterinarian

DOG CHARITIES, ORGANIZATIONS, AND RESCUE CENTERS

GREAT BRITAIN

Most of the following websites contain advice on finding a dog, caring for and training your dog, and how to find a specialist dog trainer or behaviorist.

Battersea Dogs & Cats Home
www.battersea.org.uk
The most famous rescue center in London, founded in 1860.

Blue Cross
www.bluecross.org.uk
A pet welfare charity that runs rescue centers and animal hospitals. Their website has lots of advice about looking after your pets.

Dogs Trust
www.dogstrust.org.uk
This organization runs a network of rescue centers and offers support for dog owners.

The Kennel Club
www.thekennelclub.org.uk
The organization that runs the U.K.'s national register of pedigree dogs. They officially recognize 221 dog breeds.

PDSA
www.pdsa.org.uk
The People's Dispensary for Sick Animals provides free and low-cost veterinary treatment to pets in need.

RSPCA
www.rspca.org.uk
The Royal Society for the Prevention of Cruelty to Animals is the U.K.'s largest animal welfare charity.

The Animal Behaviour and Training Council (ABTC)
abtc.org.uk
Their website can help you to find a registered dog trainer or behaviorist in your area, if your pet needs specialist help.

IRELAND

ISPCA
www.ispca.ie
The Irish Society for the
Prevention of Cruelty to Animals

Dogs Trust Ireland
www.dogstrust.ie

The Irish Blue Cross
www.bluecross.ie

USA

ASPCA
www.aspca.org
The American Society for the
Prevention of Cruelty to Animals
campaigns to promote animal
welfare. It runs shelters in New
York and Los Angeles and its
website offers a database of
rescue centers across the US.

The American Kennel Club
akc.org
The registry of dog pedigrees in
the United States. In addition,
the AKC Rescue Network can help
you find a rescue dog.

Best Friends Animal Society
bestfriends.org
Organization with a network
of shelters and rescue centers
across the U.S.

CANADA

Canadian Kennel Club
ckc.ca

PAWS Canada
www.pawscanada.org

**National Companion
Animal Coalition**
www.ncac-cnac.ca

AUSTRALIA

RSPCA Australia
www.rspca.org.au
A charity providing animal care
and protection services across
Australia. The Adoptapet service
can help you find a rescue dog.

Pet Professional Guild Australia
ppgaustralia.net.au

Pet Rescue
www.petrescue.com.au

NEW ZEALAND

SPCA New Zealand
www.spca.nz

**Association of Professional Dog
Trainers New Zealand**
www.apdtnz.org.nz

INTERNATIONAL

**Fédération Cynologique
Internationale**
www.fci.be
The FCI, or World Canine
Organization, officially
recognizes 356 dog breeds and
sets guidelines for its registered
breeders to follow.

USEFUL BOOKS

*RSPCA New Complete Dog
Training Manual*, Dr Bruce Fogle,
London: Dorling Kindersley, 2003

*The Rescue Dog: A Guide
to Successful Re-Homing*,
Vanessa Stead and Ann Stead,
Marlborough: The Crowood
Press, 2010

*The Puppy Bible: The ultimate
week-by-week guide to raising
your puppy*, Alison Smith and
Claire Arrowsmith, London:
Hamlyn, 2017

*Canine Enrichment: The Book
Your Dog Needs You to Read*,
Shay Kelly, 2019

Dog Training For Dummies,
4th edition, Wendy Volhard and
Mary Ann Rombold-Zeigenfuse,
Hoboken, NJ: Wiley, 2020

Translated from the Russian *Tvoya sobaka* by Lena Traer

First published in the United Kingdom in 2023 by
Thames & Hudson Ltd, 181A High Holborn, London WC1V 7QX

First published in the United States of America in 2023
by Thames & Hudson Inc., 500 Fifth Avenue, New York,
New York 10110

British Library Cataloguing-in-Publication Data.
A catalogue record for this book is available from
the British Library

Library of Congress Control Number 2022948756

ISBN 978-0-500-65329-6

Printed in China

Be the first to know about our new releases,
exclusive content and author events by visiting
thamesandhudson.com
thamesandhudsonusa.com
thamesandhudson.com.au

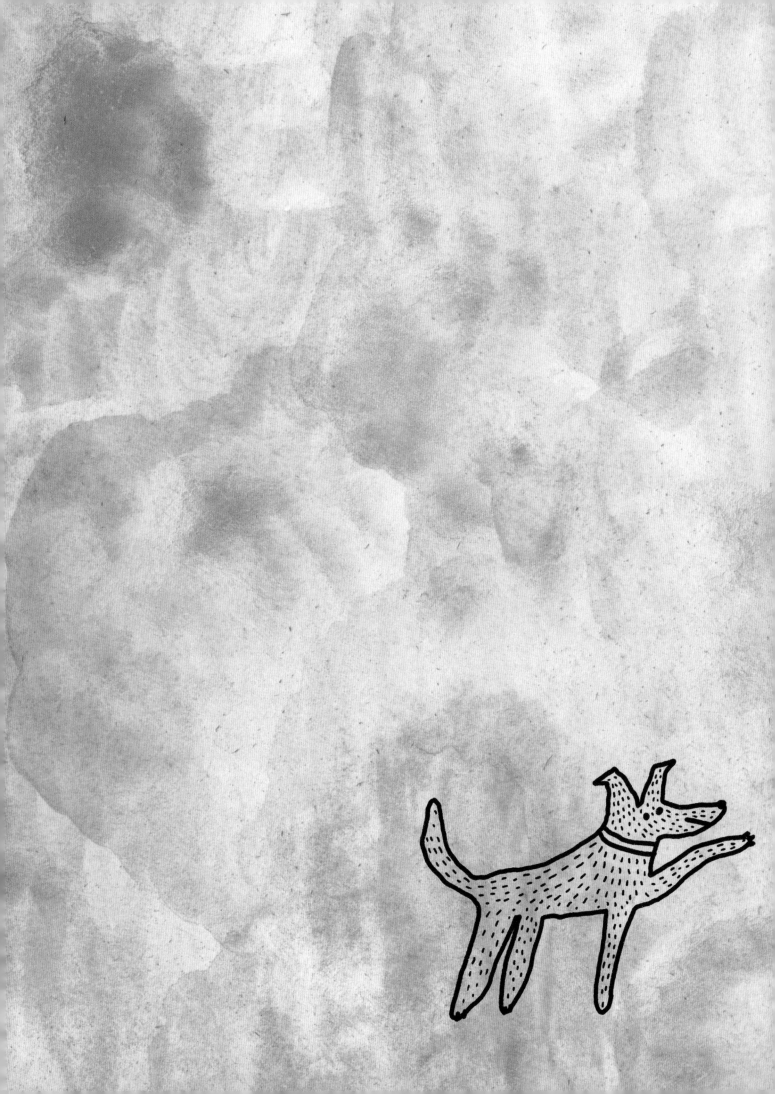